in dedication to: the ones who've touched my heart.

whether you've broken, mended, supported, and
especially loved my heart (and everything that
comes along with it), thank you for being a major
impact on my growth on becoming who I am today.

a massive thank you and all my love

♡ Joon Yambing

Life
don't dwell on this page
this is just the start
keep on reading
don't stop
discover why it's a best-seller
~ j.y

Part One

*love and other emotions: the good, the bad, and
everything in between*

tears
ironic
how something so wet
can burn like hell
~ j.y

error 404 jigsaw
maybe it's not you
I think it's me

I'm a corner puzzle piece
I feel I have two options

you
or my high expectations

and since I'm too tired
I've gone to you
and haven't even tried
to find my higher expectations

I'm not trying
and I must
so I release you
~ j.y

love is blue
the color blue
is the color of love

for love is like a tidal wave
consuming your soul

for love is like water
quenching your loneliness

for love is a state of serenity
bringing joy you've never known

mostly love is blue
like those blue suede shoes
that makes me swoon
~ j.y

are you my prince charming?
I want to like you
because you give me
the warm fuzzies,
cheeky grins
and the Flynn Rider stare

but boy
you may just be another crook
with a handsome face
ready to steal my heart

I fear I may be too late
~ j.y

toxic support
yes I want to succeed
you know what I dream
but your constant nagging
is just ripping my seams

I'm trying my hardest
to keep myself together
yet your words of good intent
actually breaks me to shards

I'm even more fragile than an eggshell
and you don't understand
I wish you did
but your closed mind has shut it out

either way I will try
but now it just hurts
to reach my goals
~ j.y

backstage of the masquerade
being emotionally exposed is the most
fragile you'll ever be
when the tears flood your face
and your voice gets cracked and breaks
you feel like you want to flee
disappear and just not be seen

but if you wipe away your fears
and look at what surrounds
you might spot someone who cares
and their face will show that
love is always around
~ j.y

intergalactic invader
why do you drag me towards your orbit?
I am my own star
but somehow
your gravitational force tries to take me away-
I don't want to be in your orbit
you're not even a part of my solar system
why are you here?
~ j.y

ghosts of ex-lovers past

why are you
back again
haunting my
every thought
I thought
you were
long gone

somehow
although
you've abandon
me
I desire your
presense
and you come

but when I
least
expect it

I should
stop wishing
you back

all you've
done is
occupy my
thoughts
and cause
confusion

I just
want to
know why haunt
me now
~ j.y

placing the public mask
breathe in
out
hold it in-
don't show
sigh off
the pain within
that wraps around
your throat
and scratches it dry
to the thumping in
your stomach
constantly making
you question
why
or the shivers
that dance and
linger in your
skin
to the dark
accessories your
eyes love to
bring
breathe in
out
don't show-
put a smile on
you're ready to go
~ j.y

dear john
your eyes pierce
through my mind
even if your
miles away I feel
your presence
harboring my bay
I don't know whether
you want me to
greet you at the docks
and bring you home
or finally say our
last goodbyes and then
I won't see you
anymore
why do you wander
and stare
why won't you speak
why don't you
leave
~ j.y

travel bug
I've decided to hop
off this train explore
the city experiencing
new senses from the
bright lights execuberated
people to the many
sights of love and
pain I know I've made
the right decision to get
off and it still
hurts the scrapes and
bruises from the fall
but I'm living life
meeting and strengthening
my relationships with
others and sometimes
I watch the train pass
by and I remember all
these sleepless nights
by your side talking
about the concepts of
words and numbers
encouraging one another
with words of hope
I miss that I can't
deny but I know the
train loop only goes
one way I don't
want that
I want to travel over borders
I want to fly
~ j.y

to the boy who thinks he might like me

I need someone who
will challenge my
ideas and motives yet
appreciate every little
quirk I possess

I need someone who
is honest and true
loves to hear
laughter escaping lips
and goodnight kisses
on cheeks

I need someone who
is unafraid to hold my hand,
hold me tight
when darkness overcomes
the light

I need someone who
will converse with me
on all topics regardless
if they're trivial or
completely serious

I need someone who
shows they care and
puts in effort to
show I matter

it's not like I'm asking
for constant I love you's
I just need to be loved
because I've loved too much
and have gotten nothing
in return

~ j.y

how's the weather colonel olsen?
the sky this morning looked like
cotton candy all fluffy
pink
blue
it was so beautiful
it tasted so sweet
but for some reason as I
sit and reminisce of the wonder of
the world's candy
I can only think of you in
your given military coat
marching down the halls
with a smirk on your
face as if you know
a secret no one knows
it makes me want to go
to you and compliment
how well boot camp treated
you and I'd tell you how
some days I taste the
sugar from above but
other times I drown
in gray but either
way I still miss the
sound of your voice saying
my name
~ j.y

free me, the mental prisoner
there's a wall that won't crumble
even as I continuously kick it down
because my heart says I'm ready
to sail the seas unending
find another island
maybe call it home
but I know I must make amends
with this last kingdom
however, that's when my brain makes me
stop

I kick and kick
and I know I can easily exit through the gates
yet I kick
only hurting myself
maybe I don't want to be
on uncharted waters
maybe I don't want to be
lost
maybe I'd rather not make amends
with the king
because I'm too afraid to see his face
and say something that may
start a battle instead

so i'm stuck kicking
unable to move
~ j.y

what is love
we glorify pain and
call it the result of
love when in truth
true love should never
break you but mend you
love lets you grow
of course people
that love you may
argue with you and
push your limits but
they only do this
because they know
that you're worth
more than all
the money in the
world and that you
have the potential
to put the stars in
your pockets. they see
the possibility of a
better future in your eyes.
they sacrifice their well-being
since they prioritize yours
oh my how you are loved
i know it's hard to see
and i guarantee it's not
like in your fairy tales
or dreams. however, this
love is real. treasure
the love you have for
you are loved
~ j.y

classic nostalgia

it's funny how strolling down
memory lane
can feel like a bus hit you
straight at your knees
or sometimes
you feel lifted on a
hot air balloon
destined for your heart's
deepest desires:
your fondest memories
and either way there's a
pang in my heart
like being shot by an arrow
and longing to live in that
moment
I miss you
I do
but I need to head
somewhere new

~ j.y

gardner, you're supposed to be kind
if you want me to grow
stop stepping on my roots
water my soil
please give me space
for the sun to touch
my face
petals won't show
if you've caused me to already
wilt
~ j.y

Sailor Boy
*"I will try to remember it was light"
vaguely the creases of your smile appear
shining through were the pearly whites of the sea
like your eyes I'd get lost in
I enjoyed the way the water reflected
the joy I felt
and I'm trying to hold on to that
but the waves grew
the tide swallowed me whole
even the glimpse of the sun
your wheat hair couldn't bring me back
I fell to the bottom
anchored by too much love
not reciprocated
I longed for fresh air
to see you
yet you've let my lungs fill
nothing grew
no flowers or jewels
so with my last bit of strength
I cut the anchor
I floated ashore
I saw your face
but I can't look at you the same anymore
however
*"I will try to remember it was light"
~j.y

*line from *"Ending With a Line From Lear"* by Marvin Bell

afloat and grounded
oh my kataline
you're my anchor in the night
never leave my side

waking to a painted sunrise
where God has splattered His
reds and yellows
the sea has mellowed
to flow to a dainty lullaby
serenading for the waves to return ashore

I continue to flow aimlessly
letting the sun's heat greet me hello
for I'm unafraid to get burned
or weighed down by young hurricane blows

because you lift me up
and encourage me to shine
you remind me that even the sky cries
and with you I feel less alone

so even when God changes His canvas
to a dark blue with purple highlights
I don't sink to the ocean floor
waiting for the day to come home

I continue to flow aimlessly
letting the moon's glow
cool me off and show
my praise

for you have been my
blessing every single day
even through the haze
~ j.y

from paris, with love
paint me like a monet
and sit with me under the comforting city lights
let your eyes tell me what your soul has been yearning

kiss me on top of the eiffel tower
paint me like a monet
let's be the reason why paris is the place for lovers to stay

even when we return home and jet-lag has passed
let your eyes tell me what your soul has been yearning
don't let our time together be only for the past

but I know you will drift like the wind
forgetting how I was your breath of fresh air as you
paint me like a monet

you'll catch me staring as if you were a blood diamond
everyone's craving
but I'll be searching if you still know my name, please
let your eyes tell me what your soul has been yearning

our time together with the european sky etched with luxe and
grandeur is long gone
but do me one last favor reminisce our time together, please
paint me like a monet
let your eyes tell me what your soul has been yearning
~ j.y

the one time I liked math
numbers were never my strongest suit
or something I had the slightest joy in using

so if I attempt to tell you what
the fundamental theorem of calculus
is or the tangent line to a curve on the graph
just know you're lucky I even tried
even when I know I'm better
with stringing the twenty six different letters
into countless forms to tell you how much I care

but for you
I'll show you how to find the slope
to my caged heart
and how you disassembled the bars
letting the fresh air renew me
or I'll show you the equation
that holds how the addition of you
in my life
divided at least fifty percent of my worries
and multiplied my happiest moments exponentially

with you every moment is an absolute value
there never is a negative

together we are limitless
headed to positive infinity
forever and always

I can't fathom subtracting you from my life
because without you I'm not whole
~ j.y

not the biggest fan of chocolate
there's a reason why our parents told us to stay away from
poison
but they never warned about how humans fit into this category

that's why I left you during spring cleaning
and every other season too
because no one needs toxic waste
clogging up their systems
rusting and molding
nothing about them can be reused

that's why people leave or you discover
it's time for someone new
one who will reinvigorate your system
make it clean and shiny
no mess to return to

sorry mama, sorry papa for not immediately listening
but now I know poisons can say your name like milk
chocolate
and make it look like you invented sunshine
now I know to watch my intake of sweets
~ j.y

***first cut is the deepest: a four poem mini-series
on my first true relationship***

have you ever had your heart so full
that you could die happy in peace
in that moment and not regret it one bit?

has anyone ever told you that your eyes
are like the sea, always changing,
yet anchoring me,
letting me have a place to call home?

your words drip out of your mouth like springtime honey
and i'm addicted to your sweetness
i crave it all day long
and at night when you kiss me softly
i can't help but smile

and when laughter spills from your lips
and your nose scrunches up and eyes crease
i can't help but smile

have you ever had your heart so full
that you could die happy in peace
in that moment and not regret it one bit?
is this what heaven feels like?

~ j.y

i was never not a fan of the day of pinks and reds
and i never complained about receiving chocolate hearts
from my so called lovers of my family and friends

but not until *you* did i realize the beauty of a valentine
soaking in the warmth of somebody at my side

the ever so often kisses on the head
or lips and cheeks and just wherever our lips met

i could cry
tears of joy of course
because i never knew i could be this happy

i've had my fair share of roller coasters of emotions
and i'm amazed i've let you break my walls
expose my heart on my sleeve
and just shown the real me to someone new

so thank you for being a sense of comfort
for making me feel beautiful
even when i struggle to be okay in my own skin

thank you for taking this chance with me
and regardless what happens for us in the future
thank you for being my first valentine
~ j.y

I've never been a fan of cliches
I've always wanted to be an original
but regardless of my wants
there's always a grain of truth
in these wishy washy platitudes

they say when someone states
after the break of a relationship
"I still want to be friends"
that all the friend they will be
is the last three letters

I believing in the best in others
hoped we wouldn't be part of the norm
that even though we used to hold hands
give each other kisses in the night's glow
we'd still be able to sit down
side by side
look into each other's eyes
knowing it's okay feelings come and go

I don't regret the time we had together
honestly I wished we had more
because even when we're feet apart
you seem an ocean afar
like the waves are blocking my voice
you're drowning and can't even see me
even when in front of you
I'm like a reflection staring back

I truly hoped we could return
to just long nights talks
discussing the validity of life out of earth
or relay our days to another

now we don't even talk or look at each other
and the thoughts keeping me up at night consist of
"if we're not friends now, were we ever at all?"

~ j.y

any relationship is a two way street
one can only do so much reaching
before their arms begins to ache
and all they can do is let go
because why keep trying
if there's no one waiting

so i've dropped my arms
and lit a match
burned this path
now i'm walking on other streets
searching for better helping hands

and no there'll be no phoenixes
rising out of the ashes
as a rebirth of what we had
reigniting the fondness and care

the road will forever be closed
i'll never return to that charred
heated direction towards you

for you had your chance to be
the second half of us

but you did nothing
didn't attempt to reach out
after my arms fell
but before the fire started

you just watched the flames
engulf what once was
admired the glow it provided
yet forgetting why it started

i didn't even say goodbye
because seems like you did
without even knowing
~ j.y

Part Two

the slump

the first step is admitting you have a problem

it's like I get these burst
of energy and I'm on a
sugar high and I
absorb all the joy
one can feel
but then
I crash and burn,
I feel so tired
I could hibernate for
years and I feel this
wave of loneliness
hit me saying
the happiness felt
wasn't even real
and I know I shouldn't
let little things impact
me so hard but
I'm just an eggshell

I break
so easily

maybe I should wander
have a sense of rebirth,
a fresh slate but breaking
has so much pain
I've endured too much

I just want sunshine
on this cloudy day
I want to feel complete
without getting high
I know I must start
loving myself
but it's hard
when no one can show
why I matter

~ j.y

the crayon box
I hate being defined
by the colors on my
skin from the yellow
covering me head to toe
marking me if I
ever go low whether
grades or my emotions
it screams
why aren't you good
I hate the black bags
under my eyes
reminding me
of so many sleepless
night consisting of my
thoughts eating away
my dreams or just
the darkness of the
world seeping into my
veins or sometimes
sore pink will adorn
my face and I can
feel so much sadness
and pain with a
tinge of anger at
this unfair world
I just want to feel
my colors not define
me but they do
I guess that's why
I never truly like
rainbows too
~ j.y

the sahara

there's too much information
swirling my mind like a
sandstrom it's eating
me up alive and all I
need is to reach the
nearest oasis and have
a sense of security
and to refresh my body,
my spirit, yet I still
wander over dunes
slowly sinking to mounds
of loneliness and despair
regardless of how loud
I cry for help no
one comes to my aid
I don't know if they're
stuck as well or just
turn the other way
when suffering is
blatant to their eyes
I hate this grab
on my life where
not even an anchor
can hold me down
and I'm constantly
choked up afraid to
speak what hurts the
most I need the
winds to calm down
so I can see that
there's ground waiting
for me so I know
I'll be alright

~ j.y

read when the bad seems greater than the good

pouring your attentions
into people and things
that make your heart
sing songs of joy
where you cry because
there's an overwhelming
amount of beauty, and
you just keep smiling
and nothing seems wrong
these are what we must
hold tightly to
when the night gets
too dark and the blackness
sucks your soul
remind yourself
there's so much to be alive for
you're not gonna want
to miss the sun breaking
through the thunder and rain
bringing back glorious smells
and sights of flowers
stay alive for the chance
you can embrace happiness
and call it your own
~ j.y

it's okay not to be okay
take a deep breath
you're not okay
assess for a way
to make yourself
not confined in
a soundproof box
crying for help
break the glass
leave the pieces
broken
just make sure
every bone in your body
the brain in your head
are properly placed
when you are free
call for help
it never hurts to have
someone
cleaning your wounds
kissing your bruises
for the truth is painted
on your skin
better they hear your words
than read the armor of flesh
cloaking your soul within
either way
find the safest path
to attain an overall
okay
~ j.y

all time low
it's not a constant lump in your throat
or waterfalls forming on your face
it's not sitting alone in a corner
wishing you'd never see the light of day
of course some days you want the sun to
swallow you up so for once
you can radiate some warmth
some life
however there are days
when laughter rings your ears
and a permanent smile appears
because you are filled with
the joy of living
but that spectrum of
up
down
is painful
the storm in your mind only destroys
you think you see the light
at the end of the tunnel
but it's actually lightning striking your
heart
you only learn to survive
each calamity when you've thirsted
paradise
when you need peace
sometimes you want to just stop caring
let the darkness take me in
~ j.y

isolated hibernation
warmth envelops my frostbitten skin
and i absorb the first bit of
comfort since the darkness closed in
i want to blend in and be unseen
under towers of sand or is it
feathers piling from overhead
shutting all noise
except only hearing my heart
beating crouched wrapped
tightly
I do not move
not even a stir
I need to persevere heat
even when I only see
the endless black hole instead
do i fear the light to
shine through?
my body is tired and can't
recall when stretched limbs
and opens hearts are needed
leave me with my mounds
of cozy misery
for at least then i can
control myself
~ j.y

Part Three

who I am / who I want to be

Matthew 5:16
for someone who is sad (a lot)
I laugh (a lot)
I do this because
laughter is one (of)
the most (beautiful) sounds
and I rather have the sound of beauty
instead of tears
I want to be a bearer of love
not fears
I want to shine
even though I feel dim
for me
laughter makes me glow
and i like the (light)
that I show
~ j.y

blooming gardens
i am nothing but the grass
always there
but never noticed
or cared for
she is the flower
bursting with joy
and beauty

you will pick her up
and I will always be stepped on
~ j.y

cosmos paint my body
I have this unnatural fascination with bruises
I get excited when I get one
I poke at it to get a feeling
and as time passes the color changes
I have this sense of awe
then once it's healed
my entertainment is over
I wait for a new
but funny
how i found beauty
in my pain
~ j.y

beyond castle walls
conforming is a double-edged sword
you can follow the ideals of truth and glory
but the other side may mock
"oh my, look at you give in"

regardless you lose parts of your identity
because even if you
listen to the beat of your drum

a new label is branded on your shoulder:
outsider

in any case,
you are not alone
~ j.y

long after blooming season
for once
I feel I've glued the vase together
the flowers can finally grow
~ j.y

truth #2
stranger starts with strange
friend ends with end
lover
ends with over
it's like the universe has destined
for people to hate one another
and for things to turn bad
but I guess I'm a believer
and I start with the only hope ever to be
~ j.y

a rose by any other name would smell as sweet
in the garden you shine so bright
radiating sweetness and might
and as you walk through all the
alluring flowers
you take notice of the yellow rose
the most peculiar of those
but you seemed enchanted
there in the garden you shine so bright
giving me hope and filling me with life
~ j.y

maybe will be okay
maybe
i hate math
because i hate numbers

for one reason
it dictates almost
everything

my future depends
on a high range of numbers
my need to learn and live
is determined by
a price tag
likes and followers
sum up to display
if you're even
appreciated
people look
at the increments
of my weight and height
and judge me

I'm not Barbie
I don't have the unfair
white advantage
where I'm entitled
to freedom
and all girls love me
I can't pull
money out of thin air
buy my way in anywhere
I'm no prodigy
who can ace
any test seen

I'm just a girl
trying to have
experiences, opportunities
yet I'm so prevented
by numbers

maybe that's why
I love poetry
~ j.y

47

how do you write in the storybook of life?
he is a pen
leaving a permanent mark
on my heart

unafraid to make
mistakes

easily moves on-

I am a pencil
obsessed with
perfection

my mark
is erasable

all I do is
stare
at my wrong

I'll never amount
as much as he
~ j.y

reminder to myself #3

you are not
the number
stating
how many people
who follow you
online

you are the
words
people say
when you walk
down the hall
alone

you are not
the GPA or test score
every college
criticized on

you are the
thoughts and
ideas you
voice out
when the world
is not fair

you are not
the places
you go

you are the
memories
you make

you are not
nothing

you are something
you are loved
you matter
~ j.y

jack pinecone
why do I hate
everything
I am-
I hate
the feeling
I need someone
to call me special
hug me tight,
kiss me at night
saying
"you are beautiful
I'm so lucky to
call you
mine"
I hate feeling
not whole
when I'm alone
although
I love my music
high or low
I'd rather
hear your
voice
singing me
a song
or just whispering
my name-
it makes me feel
insane
hating what I am
since I can't love
myself
~ j.y

spotlight

I once was so scared
of the light ahead of me
for the brightness
blinded all my sense
I was paralyzed
unknowing that if
I stepped into the
brightness and let
myself adjust
I'll bask in warmth
and realize I'm
meant for greatness
no one can stop
~ j.y

I stand with Aslan

lately I've removed high pressuring expectations
prepared for the worst
as I gather up my armor
cover my face with dirt
I fight though my battle
looking every so called enemy
in their eyes
I recognize they're like me
a human
with a life
although they may have their blade
graze my skin
and the blood starts dripping
with my soul escaping from within
I keep trudging along
sword and shield in hand
I want to get out alive
I need to be me again
with my resilience
and God's blessing protection
I see a new day
cleanse myself with pure water
passion and grace embracing me
I now understand
how to live a life

~ j.y

find yourself
sometimes we need
the contrast of
comforting ocean waves
igniting the volcano within
although we may hate
the appearance of the water
crackling amongst spews of fire
the release of tension
the state of absolute vulnerability
clears the pounding of insistent shrieks
stops the thundering commands
for you to become who you can believe in
it gives you a chance of freedom
a fresh start
as the volcanic lava sets into the sea
islands form
creating paradise and new discovery of
hope
a place where we can be
free
~ j.y

out of this world
galaxies on my skin
make me believe
I'm not from
this confined land
of tending the expectation
from others
I'm my own entity
that no one
should look down upon
but it's difficult
to grasp
that what I dream
can't always be reality
in this world
therefore I must compromise
try to burn my brightest here
while knowing in my heart
I'm meant for more
~ j.y

it's a white's world
yellow is
happiness
the sun
warmth filling your
void soul
I'm stained with
this color
asking me to conform
as a role of
being light
but don't you know
in this world
they like
it better
when the light is
white
~ j.y

olympic competition
strive for gold
ignore the silver
what is bronze?

why does this matter?

don't you see
the only thing I
see gold now is
not a string of
'A's' and 100%
I just want to see
me unstressed and
happy shining gold

I'd even gladly take
silver tears streaming
down my face over
joyous news
that I was close

give me the bronze
because at this rate it
might be the closest
thing to gold I can
reach after all the
pressure surrounding me

I want to care
in fact I do
but too much caring
too much pressure
is killing me too

(this pressure doesn't
produce diamonds)
~ j.y

here's the truth
they said love is the solution
but can't they see it's a form of destruction
wreaking havoc into everything

you can care too much
forgetting the truth
who are you
what are you fighting for

it blinds you with its seducing light
and when you finally open your eyes
bitter sorrow seeps into your insides
invading your veins
filling your lungs with acid rain

you may argue
this is rejection
but you don't understand
I am the embodiment of love
I have sacrificed
given up my prized organ
letting it shatter along with my hope

the beat of my drum
has turned into a distress call
for tragedy

as they say love is war

and with my heart ripped off my sleeve
my mind is now the only thing that thinks

now this is my truth
~ j.y

Vulnerability
I keep my arms covered
because I am afraid
the sun will burn
my heart on my sleeve
yet exposure
is what I need
to breathe
~ j.y

golden rampage

it's sixteen minutes after midnight
I'm wide awake
I'm burning gold
melting frozen icicles swords
aimed for my throat

and my heart is ready
to rampage
to own this sleepless city

I'm enveloped in the darkness' cape
it's nearing dawn
but I'm burning gold
I pick up my worn out paint brush
dip it in faint glitter
and start splashing
the blanket canopy of the earth

and my heart is leaping
sprinting
beginning
to rampage

I'm finally alive
I'm finally ready to make this life
mine
I have risen with the sunrise
~ j.y

*"The flower that blooms in adversity is the most rare and
beautiful of all"
dark lavender flower in sandy dunes
how can I complain
when somehow a drop of heaven decides to grow
in hell's touch on earth

I want to be seen the same
as the lone bloom
defeating adversity
despite what others believe
I've trekked up the highest mountains
not even everest can compare
crossed the most dangerous seas
where waves were more hungrier than
possible sharks swimming in it's haunted lairs

let me be the first and only one to say
I'm giving my all
trust me

grand pianos continue to drop
I engulf the raucous melodies
although the pressure may kill me
but that's where I feel I can be my own sun
lighting up my own solar system

I'm going to keep living this way
if I'm able to withstand the turmoil
yet still produce beauty
I will
because how can I complain
when I'm a drop of heaven deciding to grow
in hell's touch on earth
~ j.y

*line from the movie *Disney's Mulan* said by Fa Zhou

*the roots of a wildflower have been established.
time to watch her grow*

my mission statement
I want to
experience the
world
and capture its
soul
and help people
realize they're
worth more than
gold
I want to find
beauty in everything
whether from your
voice saying 3 words
or 2 instead-
or by
the way the sky
puts up a new
canvas for display overhead
I hope people
see me as
a flower growing
among weeds
as I help pollinate
the Earth
with kindness
and good deeds
bringing color to
life
being a sign of
joy to all
I want people to
think they matter
so I can start
thinking I am too
~ j.y

Made in the USA
San Bernardino, CA
24 August 2017